Room

The First Thanksgiving

Lou Rogers

Illustrations by Michael Lowenbein

Follett Publishing Company   *Chicago · New York*

Library of Congress Catalog Card Number: 62-8711

FIFTH PRINTING   TLA 2884

Many, many years ago some people who
called themselves Pilgrims left England to find
a new home. Pilgrims were people who went to
far away places for religious reasons.

These Pilgrims wanted to have their own
churches. But the King of England would not
let them have their own churches. He said that
the Pilgrims must go to his church.

"We will not stay here," the Pilgrims said.
"We will go to Holland, where people are free
to go to their own churches."

So they went to Holland.

Holland is a beautiful country. It has clean cities and many flowers.

It has many rivers and canals. It has walls, called dikes, to keep the water from covering the low land.

In winter, when the canals freeze over, children and grownups skate on the ice.

The Pilgrims were hard workers, and they
soon found work. But they were country people,
and in Holland they had no land. They had to
do city work.

Even the children had to work, for the
Pilgrims were very poor.

The Pilgrim mothers and fathers said, "We
do not want our children to work for other
people all their lives in a strange city. We
do not want them to run away to be soldiers or
sailors.

"We must find a place to live where more
people will come from England, or our children
will lose our ways and our church will die."

The Pilgrims knew about a new land far
across the ocean. It was called America.
Some of it belonged to England.

"We will go to America," they said. "There is much land in America. We can build our own town. We can go to our own church. Our children can be English children."

The Pilgrims got on a ship. It was named the *Speedwell*.

The *Speedwell* took them to England. Other Pilgrims and some other English people who wanted to go to America met them in England. They were on a ship named the *Mayflower*. The two ships sailed off for America.

The *Speedwell* was not strong enough for the big ocean waves. The water came through the bottom of the ship. The *Speedwell* had to go back to England, and the *Mayflower* went back too.

Many of the people on the *Speedwell* got on the *Mayflower*. Soon they left England and the town of Plymouth far behind.

The *Mayflower* had sails. The wind blowing on the sails made the ship go. The *Mayflower* sailed on and on across the ocean.

The children thought they would never get to America.

The ship was very crowded. There were 102 people besides the sailors.

The 31 children played games on the decks.
On the ship was a small boat, like a fishing
boat. It was on the upper deck. It made a good
place for the children to hide.

Sometimes the children got in the way of
the sailors. Then Captain Jones made them go
down into the big cabin. They could not play
there. It was too crowded.

Captain Miles Standish was an army captain.
He was the only soldier on the *Mayflower*.
Captain Standish had to teach the men how to fight.

When the men came up on the deck to drill,
the children had to be quiet. It was fun to
watch the men drill. When the drill was over,
the children played soldier.

The sea was very rough. Sometimes the
waves washed over the decks. Once a bad storm
almost turned the ship over.

The weather got colder and colder, and the
people had to stay in the cabin. The air in
the cabin was bad. Many of the people got sick.

At last the Pilgrims could see land. They
were very happy.

The *Mayflower* sailed into Cape Cod Bay.
This was a place where the ocean cut into the
land. The land made a curve around the ocean.
The waves were not as high in the bay as on
the open ocean.

But the Pilgrims needed a place where the land was good for growing crops. They needed a place where there was deep water for the ship close to the land.

Captain Miles Standish and some of the men got in the small fishing boat. They sailed along the coast looking for a good place. A storm came, and the men thought they would all be drowned.

After three trips in the small boat, the men found a harbor that was deep enough for the *Mayflower*. They found fields where the Indians had planted corn. There was good water for drinking.

The men went back to the *Mayflower* with
the good news. Soon after that, the ship
sailed into the harbor. The people went ashore.

They called the place where they landed
Plymouth, after the English town of Plymouth.

The Pilgrims had to live on the ship for
many more days. They had to live there while
the men cut down trees and built houses.

The weather was cold, much colder than it was in England. There was not enough food to last through the winter. Many of the people got sick.

It was a hard time for the Pilgrims. Only one half of them lived until spring came.

One day an Indian came to Plymouth. His
name was Samoset. He could say some English
words. Samoset brought other Indians to meet
the Pilgrims. He brought Massasoit, the chief
of the Indians. The governor of Plymouth and
Chief Massasoit agreed that the Indians and the
Pilgrims would be friends and help each other.

With Chief Massasoit came Squanto. Squanto
had been to England with some sailors. He could
talk English. Squanto lived with the Pilgrims.

Squanto was a good friend. He showed the
Pilgrims where to fish and how to plant corn.
He told them to plant the corn seeds with dead
fish. The fish made the soil better so that
the corn grew well.

The Indian corn was very important. The
seed the Pilgrims brought from England did not
grow well. They made bread out of corn.

When spring came, Captain Jones said, "I must sail back to England in the *Mayflower*. Who would like to go with me?"

Not one of the Pilgrims went back. They were brave people.

"We will not go back," the Pilgrims said. "We will stay here and work hard. Some day things will be better."

When fall came, things were better. The
Pilgrims had homes. They had all the food they
could eat.

Governor Bradford said, "God has been good
to us. We have homes, and we have food. We
can go to our own church. We should thank God
for all these things."

The people said, "Yes, we must thank God,
for He has been good to us. Set a day for us
to come together and thank Him. We will have a
feast and invite our Indian friends."

Governor Bradford set a special day of
thanksgiving. He invited the Indians.

The men went hunting. They shot wild turkeys in the woods. They shot deer.

Some of the men went fishing.

The women baked many good things to eat. They cooked most of the things in their big fireplaces. The men cooked the deer over a fire outside.

The children fished. Some of them dug clams. Some of them gathered wood for the fires. Others gathered berries, nuts, plums, and wild grapes.

Some of the boys gathered cranberries.
The cranberries grew on vines in low wet places.
They were hard to get, but they were good to
eat with turkey when they were cooked.

At last Thanksgiving Day came. The
Pilgrims went to church first. They thanked
God because He had been so good to them.

Then they went home to the feast.

The Indians came to the feast. There were
90 Indians. The Pilgrims and Indians sat down
at long tables. The tables were out under the
trees. The children and some of the Indians
sat on the grass.

There was enough good food for everybody.
They had deer, turkeys, geese, ducks, fish, and
clams. They had corn, beans, squash, pumpkins,
plums, grapes, nuts, cranberries, and corn cakes.

After dinner they had fun. The Indians
did a dance. They showed how well they could
shoot with their bows and arrows.

Captain Standish marched his men and boys
on parade. The children ran races and played
games. The boys played ball.

The Indians had such a good time that
they did not want to leave. They stayed for
three days.

Chief Massasoit sent some of the Indians
into the woods. They came back with five deer.

It is a long time since the Pilgrims
thanked God for helping them in a new country.
Their new country is now the United States of
America. Americans in many states have held
Thanksgiving every fall since the time of the
Pilgrims.

President Abraham Lincoln set a special
day for Thanksgiving and said it should be held
each year all over the country. Now every year
the fourth Thursday in November is Thanksgiving
Day.

All over the country, people gather their
families together and have a feast. They thank
God for the good things of the past year. They
eat turkey. They remember the brave Pilgrims
and the first Thanksgiving Day.

Follett Beginning Social Studies Books

Follett Beginning Social Studies books contain accurate, up-to-date information about our world — its history and geography, its people and their ways of life. These books are designed to provide pleasure in reading and to give children the information they need to enrich their lives and their school work.

Follett Beginning Social Studies books are written for the primary grades. They are completely illustrated. They cover a wide range of subjects, adding interest to the familiar and shedding light on the unfamiliar.

The First Thanksgiving

Understandings Developed in This Book

Who the Pilgrims were.

The Pilgrims were English people who did not want to follow the ways of the Church of England.

Why the Pilgrims left England.

In England, everyone was supposed to belong to the Church of England. Those who worshipped God in other ways were punished.

Why the Pilgrims came to America.

There was plenty of land in America. The Pilgrims could own land and have their own town. They could make their own laws and worship God as they thought right. Their children would have a chance for a better life.

What the voyage on the Mayflower was like.

It took a long time to get to America from England (two months). During this time the Pilgrims were very crowded on the tiny ship. There was no heat, and the weather was very cold. The sea was rough, and there were many bad storms.

How the Pilgrims lived during the first year.

It was nearly winter when the Pilgrims landed in America. They had to build houses, for the weather was very cold. They did not have enough food. More than half the people got sick and died.

How the Indians helped the Pilgrims.

The Indians taught the Pilgrims how to live in the new country. They showed them where to fish and how to plant corn. Without the Indians the Pilgrims might have starved.

What the Pilgrims had to be thankful for.

After their first harvest, the Pilgrims had enough food for the winter. They had houses to live in. Though half of them had died during the first winter, those that remained were strong and healthy. They had made friends with the Indians. They were free to worship as they thought right.

Why we honor the Pilgrims.

The Pilgrims were willing to work hard and brave great dangers rather than do what they thought was not right. Because of their beliefs they crossed the stormy ocean in a tiny ship. They suffered hunger and sickness through the first winter, but still they remained to make homes in the new land.

Words That May Be New

Pilgrims	Speedwell	Bay	cranberries
England	Mayflower	harbors	squash
religious	Plymouth	Samoset	United
reasons	Miles	Massasoit	States
church	Standish	governor	President
Holland	Cape	Squanto	Abraham
English	Cod	Bradford	Lincoln